This book is dedicated to my mother Fran. I love you mom.

Table of Contents

COPYRIGHT PAGE

INTRODUCTION

There are lots of customer service books on the market for business owners. The lack of advice and support for small business owners in the service industry was one thing that caught my attention.

Many of the books on the market appear to concentrate more on "white collared" and do not cover the rotting beam under your customers home that was not caught in the original estimate or to how to deal with one of your "rougher" blue-collar employees steal something from one of your Customers during a household shift.

The ups and downs of service businesses with clients can be quite traumatic. Our "roughneck" teams can produce customer service problems from landscapers to concrete crews that anyone in a white collared shirt and tie will never understand.

In this guide, I will talk about real-life customer service problems that I have experienced with some of my businesses. Over the years I have owned several moving companies, carpet cleaning companies, and even remodeling firms.

I have had Employee pass away on my customer's floor during a move and I have had box trucks trapped under bridges in New York City with the roof ripped off and $100,000 in damage to the bill.

I will teach you how to deal with common scenarios that happen in the service industry, how to deal with credit card back charges, items missing from customers' homes, property damage complaints, and more.

We both know I could write an encyclopedia on the issues that can arise in owning a service business. While I use real-life complaints that I have and my employees have dealt with over the year, I would like if you could think of the theory of customer service. You must know your customer, what is important to them, and how to prevent customer issues by knowing and understanding your employees before they occur.

I hope that you can use this book to improve your overall view of the customer, be able to maintain near-perfect reviews, and help relieve yourself, your staff, and the customer from customer stress.

For over two decades, I have been working for myself and I can assure you that I have confidently grown to where I am today. In my first years in business, my views on customer service were null. I am embarrassed and would avail this opportunity to apologize to any customer I yelled at, insulted, or felt threatened by my demeanor. I was unprofessional and there was no excuse for my actions.

Ten years later, I can assure you that I am entirely a new man. I went from ignoring and blocking customer phone calls to personally reaching out to customers during my company's work to ensure everything was right.

And guess what, it feels so much better. Let me be honest, if I heard what I am pitching 12 years ago I would have laughed and said it was some bull shit some college kids in an office came up with.

Let me help you right now. Business is not about having a CEO in your email signature, neither is it about having an LLC or INC after your business name or having company box seats at the local hockey rink.

Business is about money for most of us when we enter the field and ideally, as you expand, it will be about your employees and your clients. However, if your focus on business is just about money, then you should read every word in this book and follow it through. If you do, I can assure you that your revenue and profits will increase after you push through the lull of your current level of service.

What are the advantages of being "obsessed with your customer experience," as Jeff Bezos would say?

- Huge increase in revenue and profits
- Spend less on advertising and make your reputation more stable
- Able to charge more for your services than your competitors
- Decrease employee turnover by creating a better work environment
- Sleep better at night

If you feel like it is too late, do not worry, we can fix this together. Take a minute and look yourself in the mirror. Tell yourself you can do this. You can fix this.

Once you become a Customer Service Beast the joy from solving your customers' problems and supporting your Employees to work through them will become just as rewarding as scheduling a big job or cashing a big check.

You will gain more wealth if you can attract more customers. And good service will help you attract more customers.

What are your expectations when you hire a service business to work at your home?

An important part of understanding how to be at the top of your game when it comes to Customer Service is to build and execute a customer service mission connected with a customer service process.

In an age of online reviews and social recommendations, small business owners walk a fine line when it comes to protecting the reputation of our means of livelihood.

A big part of creating a great customer experience is to put yourself in the customer's shoes. Think and even write down what you expect when someone is providing you a service.

Create a list of the issues you have experienced with a service provider that has frustrated you or cost you time and money.

- When the AC Guy continues to postpone his appointment and then reschedules the next day, costing me a whole day of productivity.

- When my mover's I hired pants were hanging off they're rear-ends looking horrible and making myself, my children, and my wife uncomfortable.

- Answers the phone by just saying: "Hello"

- When the Septic Pump company leaves a huge rut on my lawn leaving and squashes a sprinkler head deeper into the lawn

- When the fence guy cut the cable to our tv when digging the post holes

- Running over a nail in the driveway left by the roofers

- 15 minutes late for an appointment

Over the years, I have had a few homes and have had my fair share of experiences with my service businesses based in those communities.

Some of the things on my list might not seem like a big deal to me, and most days they are not. Some things happen I possibly exaggerate a little because I am in the business of Customer Service, but for the most part, I am fair and just. The list is long, and I could probably go on for pages about other not-so-perfect experiences I have had with different service businesses.

I have learned that it is important to understand what bothers me so that I can have empathy for others going for the same thing.

When what bothers you is fresh in your mind, it will help you have a stronger emotional connection with your customer.

The facts are true. I looked at Google reviews in my local area, I picked a few trades and counted the total within 12 miles of my home and the total of these service providers who had a Google reputation score of 4 Stars or higher.

Service Type	Total Providers	Total with over 4 Stars
Lawn Maintenance	44	6
Carpet Cleaners	51	11
Movers	29	4
Locksmiths	40	3
Masons	4	0

What does this chart teach us? This chart reveals huge opportunities to grow a business in any of these businesses. There is a significant number of customers looking for great service. Think about how hard you work for your money. Would you hire someone with 2.8 stars rating on Google or someone with 4.3 stars? I think we both know there is a good chance that even if the price of the 2.8-star company is cheaper, it will probably still end up costing more time, headaches, and money than just originally would have hired the 4.3-star provider.

Have you ever heard the saying "treat others like you would like to be treated"?

This is a simple rule in the customer service part of your service business. Think about how you would like to be treated if the problem your customers are presenting to you was your problem.

Think about the stress from losing the money yourself, or another two days without air conditioning, or another week with long hedges your HOA keeps complaining about. Your customers' problems are your problems and owning this will make you a much more financially successful and loveable small service business owner.

Who, where and why is your Customer your Customer?

I noticed that small service business owners have a major challenge with regards to the lifestyles and needs of their customers.

To ensure you are providing the best service, you must understand your customers and how they carry themselves. While some customers will appreciate your low prices and willingness to haggle, others will be put off and anxious.

I remember living in a $100,000 house thinking I understood what my customers in their million-dollar homes wanted. Where I would cheap out on this or that service to save a few bucks, (or fix it myself) it seemed to them like I was just cutting corners and settling for less.

Significantly lower your prices, cutting materials or parts from a service that may save money now but can cause problems later will only hurt you. Avoid putting a low value on the services you provide. Focus on delivering the best service with high-quality work, and you will be able to charge higher prices.

In many of my service businesses, I have learned to "evolve" through my customers. I have learned to "evolve" through my clients in many of my service businesses. For example, when I first got into the moving business in 2009, I advertised heavily on Craigslist and most of my customers paid cash. At that time, my rate for two men was $40 for two helpers. Two years later, I stopped advertising on Craigslist, we stopped accepting cash and we introduced a deposit policy that allowed you to secure your appointment with a credit card before the movers even showed up.

Guess what happened to my business? It grew exponentially and the same 2 Man crew 18 months later was now billing at $99 per hour for a two men crew. The team's weekly revenue grew by over 100%, the customers we used were easier to deal with and seemed less restricted by budget and more focused on having things done the right way.

Am I saying it is a bad idea to do business on Craigslist? Not. What I am saying is, that is especially important to know your customers and grow and evolve your customer base.

Believe it or not the customers I evolved into were more focused on quality questions when hiring me rather than money questions. It has a huge effect on your day.

There are two important components to nailing down a strategy for retaining the customers you want:

1. What type of Customer do you consider to be ideal?
2. What does the data reveal about who your real customer is?

Who do you believe is your target market? For instance, in my carpet cleaning businesses, I would think that my ideal customer would be people who own homes worth more than $500,000.

Turns out quite the contrary as I run the data. My customers turned out to live in homes worth between $250k and $500k, with 85% of them being a woman. My customers were mostly located in the suburbs, with just a few in the downtown metro. It was funny because I thought I had more jobs downtown. After all, those jobs stuck in my mind more. After all, they settled on my mind more.

Knowing this information from just going over the data from the last few months would assist me in deciding who my customer is. And sometimes, like in the instance of the carpet cleaning business, it would be difficult to make the same profits if I focused only on Men that lived in homes of $1 million or more.

That is what I would call over-evolving your ideal customer. The data for the most part will assist you to identify who the customer is and where they came from. Knowing this would allow you to reduce acquisition costs and produce more revenue and profits.

How to figure out **your** ideal customer

1. Collect data from your last 30-60 jobs (at least two months' worth of data is a good control).

2. If you have a CRM, you maybe be able to run custom reports. If you do not have that option, get a paper and pen and get ready to start crunching. Many of these have a source option, which will help you measure your return on advertising investment.

3. Organize your Work Orders into different categories so you can concentrate on who your Current customer is. Men and women should be segregated, and job locations map should be printed from your CRM or grouped by location.

After that, you want to answer the following questions (I will continue to use my Carpet Cleaning company as an example)
1.What services did they use?
2. How much is the house worth?
3. What sources brought them to me?
4. How many of my customers are Male or Female?
5. Did one source produce higher ROI for the customers cultivated from that source?
6. Am I able to group them young, middle-aged, or older? (checking social profiles or from your memory of that customer)

Going through my last 100 jobs (about two months of work) I learned the following information about my customer: My average ticket from all sources combined is $167.50. My highest price per ticket source is Google Local Ads (see my other books to learn more about Google Local Ads).

My average customers are middle-aged women who live in homes worth $278,000 or more. These Customers tend to find me the most through Google Local and they call in live more than they email or submit quotes. This Customers with the highest ROI usually schedules on a weekday and they are located on the inside of the Interstate Loop with a high concentration on the east side of town.

So, now that I have narrowed down the who and where (which takes me half a day of work), the next thing I should know is why my customers use me. This may seem like a simple question as many of my customers come to me to have their carpets cleaned.

If you dig deeper on the why you might come up with some reasons why by just thinking back to why you hired whatever service business, you hired to work on your home. Perhaps you, like me, came up with some of the same reasons for hiring someone.

1. Let us go over some of the "whys" we would expect a service provider to come to our house. They had a strong online presence with good great reviews.

2. They were easy to communicate with over the phone.

3. I heard good things about them from a buddy who used them.

I have seen them before in my neighborhood. What are some good "Whys" the companies I hired should strive to focus on based on my list above?

1. Make sure they keep a clean website and manage a good reputation
2. Make sure my calls are clear, answered professionally with no background noise
3. If they perform good work, they will get more work from word of mouth
4. Using a company vehicle with a well-branded logo and passing door hangers to the neighbors of a job site will generate work.

Knowing that these same "Whys" are important to my Carpet Cleaning Busines or Moving Company allows me to concentrate even more on who my customer is and devote more attention to that aspect of my business. So now that I've gotten answers to the "Whys," I can change my previous statement to:

My Customers are typically middle-aged women who live in homes worth $278,000 or more. These Customers tend to find me the most through Google Local where I have perfect reviews, and they prefer to call rather than email or send quotes. Knowing that my main Customer likes to call in, we must have a respectful conversation. This Customers with the highest ROI usually schedules on a weekday and they are located on the inside of the Interstate Loop with a high concentration on the east side of town.

It is impossible to fail by concentrating your efforts on your most valuable customers. When a service problem occurs, it is easier to communicate with and relate to these Customers if you know who they are.

You will notice that your ideal or most frequent customers have problems or concerns that are similar in scale. Knowing your customer and their needs will help you avoid having to deal with customer service problems and more importantly train you how to relate better to new customer service issues that are guaranteed to rise.

What role do your employees play in the experience of your customers?

If you purchased this book, you already know there is a problem that needs to be solved. Over the years, I have had both good and poor employees in many of my small service companies. One thing I have learned is the importance of directly tying your Employees into the Customer service experience.

Empowering your Employees requires you to have one on one talks with Employees when Customers say something directly or through a survey about an Employee. How that Employee reacts and grows will tell you a lot about what you must work or change completely with that Employee.

Bad attitudes cannot be tolerated, and this includes the business owners themselves. I cannot even count how many times I handled myself wrong with an Employee and how embarrassed I was afterward. You are the only person in your small business who has the power to set the tone for who you are as a company.

You will need to have all your employees on the same page if you are trying to incorporate these new strategies into an established business. A few group meetings, where you explain the company's new outlook on customer service and encourage them to ask questions and give feedback are only going to make the long ride smoother.

You must communicate with your Employees constantly about what is going on. Over the years, I have discovered the importance of getting to know my employees. Knowing their personal and professional backgrounds helps us develop as a team, minimize employee turnover, and improve income for my company.

I cannot tell you how many small business owners I have met over the years have failed miserably because, despite having the resources and understanding the administrative and marketing aspects, they had no connection with their customers or employees.

If you bury your head in the sand from your Customers and Employees, it will show in your available bank balance. Employees in the service business who work in the field are more resistant to change than those in my office who work in the air conditioning all day. In the early years of business, you might find yourself with a "rough bunch" that are willing to mow lawns in the heat all day or clean carpets in the cold. In these meetings, you want to share who your Customer is and what they expect. Make a list of 5-10 of the most recent customer service issues. You can go through the last 20-50 complaints and count how many of the same or similar complaints there are.

Next to the most common complaints write down why it may have happened that way and what we can do to prevent this in the future. Do not use Customer or Employee names when you go through your most common complaints; the last thing you want is for one of your employees to become defensive and then take it out on a potential customer. In this next example, I will use my Moving Company to list out the most common complaints we have received and how we intend to avoid them in the future. This chart becomes part of your Customer Service Process and should be documented and distributed to everyone involved in the process.

Common Problem	Why	How to prevent
Late for appointment	Traffic to the job, Employee Late	Instead of exact arrivals change the arrival time to a one-hour window (8 am-9 am)
Scratches on floors	Movers having dirt and stones in their shoes can cause damage on floors	Purchased floor runners for all the teams and had Team Leads upload pictures of any floor damage before starting the job
Bill was higher than expected	The customer said over the phone that they would get more work completed than they would, which resulted in more work for us.	Send confirmation emails and text messages that provide a cost estimate. We began presenting our estimates as a range, so instead of $900 for the move, it now says approximate costs of $900-$1200.
Mover not working hard enough told Customer it was his first day	That is crew	Send any new guys as a third mover at no charge until Team Manager approves. This also will save us on damage claims.
Damage to dressers	Not fully blanket wrapping dressers	Had our movers upload a picture of any pre-damages then of

piece fully wrapped. This prevents our Team from saying the damage was there with no physical documentation to prove otherwise.

Knowing my crew and their capabilities was crucial in coming up with solutions to my common problems. Most of my employees commute to work in a shared vehicle or by Uber. To say everyone must be here on time or they are reprimanded might not work out for the current life situation of many of my field workers.

Why won't it work out? Because I know my Team and their capabilities. I am going to get an employee profile in the moving industry for the pay scale and type of work I will be doing.

My customer only complained about us being late because we set the expectation of what time we would be thereby. So, moving ahead, we set 1-hour arrival windows and got no pushback from customers, and I kept my solution in line with my Crew's expectations. After that, I went from 5-10 customers calling at 8:08 a.m. searching for their team to just 1-2 customers calling once a month.

When we discuss the process of great customer service later in this book, I will show you how we make a Complaint Tracking Form. This form would include a section for the names of employees involved in any part of the job's operation. You or your operations manager will then meet with the employees and get their version of events and discuss how this could be presented in the future.

Another important part of the process would be a follow-up with the employees on how the company solved the problem. For this part of the process, I would send out a less invasive text message to the employee at the end of the day (do not set a bad mood if the Employee takes the text message the wrong way). Here is an example of a text message I would send:

"Good afternoon Talha, I just wanted to let you know we got the dresser fixed and Mrs. Smith is happy again. It cost a little over $100 to get that fixed, so if you could please take pictures of pre-existing damages before touching that item in the future, that would be great. Mr. Jackson gave you a glowing review yesterday, saying, I appreciate your hard work and glad we worked this out together".

I would also encourage my management team to track complaints per employee on a spreadsheet. This helps us know what we needed to work on with the Employee from a training standpoint and what the complaints were costing the company in hard costs.

You will notice the number of complaints drops, and you will never have to worry about any of them because you will entrust your employees to handle minor and common complaints where they are capable.
You are probably saying to yourself, "There's no way that will work with my people." You may expect them to laugh or roll their eyes in response. Hey, if that happens, you will know exactly where to begin fixing the problem.
I have had some of the roughest crews you can imagine from Storm Chasers to Movers I had quite the Team. I found that the rougher I thought an Employee was, the easier it was to get them excited about better service.

If the employees feel rewarded, they would be more enthusiastic about providing excellent service. With my moving company, the reward was the mover's tips as credit cards increased by almost 40% in a noticeably short time. At the same time, I made more profits and spent less time trying to fix Customer Service issues.

The half-empty part of me needs to warn you that not everyone can understand it, do it, or be enthusiastic about it. This is where you, as an Owner will decide a lot about the future of your service business.

If you have that guy who is mechanically inclined and edges lawns better than you, but whenever he meets a customer, there is an issue, it is time to review. Is the bad attitude worth it?

Was I concerned that this employee would cause customers to cancel their orders? Will new or other Employees get this same attitude.

You need to know and set a good tolerance level. Let us face it, some people have bad days, bad weeks, bad months, and as far as 2020 went even better years. There will come a time when you know that keeping the team you have, training and working with them, will yield better results than hiring and firing, which seems to be the norm in most small service businesses.

Also, avoid putting too much Customer Stress on Employees. There is a balance for every different operation.

Take a picture and text it to employees when they get a positive rating with their name on it. Acknowledging the good in your Tea makes getting through the bad that much easier.

You must realize that it will take equal efforts from yourself, your customers, and your employees to make this work. You need to support your Employees and they need to support your vision when working for you. The balance is there, I promise you it is.

What is fair to you if something goes wrong?

How you plan on dealing with complaints and issues is important in creating a realistic mission and process for your service business. How you deal with issues that arise overall is important. When dealing with issues you need to be fair and reasonable. Remember the final goal is profits but you should also strive to be less stressed over customer service issues.

How will you deal with things when they go wrong? Will you try and talk your way out of it, throw money at it, or meet your customer face to face. This section is for you to make sure your Customer Service goals are within what you can tolerate. Let us look at different solutions to different problems.

Let start with an example; I was recently looking for a new scuba mask. I ordered a mask from Amazon because I was trying to stay Covid-19 safe by not going to my local dive shop. When the mask arrived, I tried it on and it was a disaster. With a click of a button, a label is printed, and UPS came to my house the next day to pick it up.

Following that, I went to my local dive shop in the hopes of getting a new mask in time for my dive trip. My budget was around $100. I was able to find the perfect fitting mask after trying on about a dozen different models after spending time with the salesperson who also happened to be a diver. I ended up paying nearly twice as much as I had expected, but I felt the service was commensurate.

That coming weekend, I go on my dive and not even five minutes in the strap snaps. I see from the design that the strap is right on the edge of a metal clasp. It is a design flaw and the only way to get around it is by bringing the metal tab around to the backside where it would dig directly into the back of my head. I put that mask back in my bag, grab my old mask and enjoy the rest of the weekend spearfishing and eating.

That following week I get settled back at home. By Thursday I have some free time, I cannot find the original box, so I grab the mask and the mask bag it came with and drive the thirty minutes over the dive shop. When I arrive, there is a sign hanging on the door that says, "Be back in 15 minutes, had to go to Post Office". I am a little annoyed and fool around on my smartphone for 20 minutes".

The salesperson who arrives is not the same as my previous salesperson, and he seems annoyed to see me waiting outside his shop door. He passes by, opens the door, and walks in without saying anything. I follow behind him with mask and bag in tow standing there waiting for an acknowledgment. "Can I help you?" he eventually asked, more in an I must tone than and I want to tone.
I told him my story and showed him the strap. Without even acknowledging my story, he inquiries about the box and informs me that there will be a 15% restocking charge if the box is not returned. I have lost any motivation to look for another mask, collected my money minus the 15% restocking charge, and drove the 30 minutes back home.

Let us look at this story and see what could go different. Am I expecting the local dive shop to compete with Amazon? No way. What I am expecting is good service and compassion for the trouble of having to return the time. Amazon would be able to provide good service as far as the return of the item, but Amazon was not there helping me try on lots of masks with lots of knowledge. Another advantage that small businesses have over big businesses is compassion. Having compassion for your customers and their issues is priceless.

What are ways this could have gone different?

- The return policy should have been explicitly stated on my receipt and possibly somewhere in the store,
- The first salesperson had a great personality, so great that it was a real downer on my return trip
- The Employee should have apologized for the inconvenience, "I'm so sorry, I hope this didn't ruin your dive"
- And followed that up with: "There is a 15% restocking fee but let's take a look at a coupe mask that I can recommend, and they are a little more cost-effective than the one you have in your hand."

Big Corporations are not putting small businesses out of business. Several small businesses do extremely well. I can assure you that a customer would rather call a local area code when looking for a locksmith rather than calling an 800? There are a few reasons I think that customers are willing to pay more to local small businesses

- The personal connection is especially important to customers
- Some may think since your smaller, you have lower overhead and will be cheaper, (on the contrary its quite the opposite larger companies can spread their cost by suing volume, something a local service business has a hard time obtaining)
- People despise hold music and calling into an *800 Sales line for a company that offers service usually starts with having to press menu buttons, voice recognition systems that mess up, and taking twice as long as you expected to take to purchase the actual service
- The consumer can appreciate the management aspect of not being moved around to a variety of departments if anything goes wrong.

Maybe the solution to a problem for the local dive shop was a 15% restocking fee due to overhead. That solution turned into a customer service issue, so it does not seem like it was a great solution. Remember your solutions are going to have a lot of what you can tolerate.

Some examples of problems that can have multiple solutions depending on the owner and personality

Problem	Solution 1	Solution 2	Solution 3
About 30 minutes late for an appointment, the Customer calls looking for Team.	Have the Team Manager call and explain	Have the owner or manager call the customer and apologize	Call and offer the Customer $15 off today's service for the inconvenience
Scuffed and fist-size indented sheetrock damage reported by an Employee	Call the Customer immediately and let them know you will have it repaired. Let them know your handyman will reach out to get this fixed	Call and offer the Customer $30 off from their service to cover the costs of the damages	Tell the Employee not to worry about it
Customer completes a survey and says they did not feel like they got value	Look over the job details and all the customers. Decide before the call if	Look over the job details and all the customers. Decide	Call the Customer and let them vent. Apologize profusely, let the Customer

from the service	there was value and if the Customers reasons make sense. If it does, offer them a $165 refund to get them back closer to their original estimate	before the call if there was value and if the Customers reasons make sense. If it does, offer them a $50 refund and a future credit of $50.	know you will use this as a training exercise.

Take a moment after viewing this chat to write out solutions to any issues you may encounter. Try and come up with a few different solutions to a problem. After you complete that, imagine you are the Customer with the issue you have listed. Be honest with yourself and pick which one would satisfy you. I am over the top pro customer service and many of my business-owner friends think I give away and give back too much money. Of course, I have 4.6 or higher ratings at all my companies that do million a more per year even though we all started as one persona owner-operated operations.

These are the solutions I can tolerate and would pick.

Problem	Solution 1	Solution 2	Solution 3
About 30 minutes late for appointment, Customer calls looking for Team.	Have the Team Manager call and explain	Have the owner or manager call the customer and apologize	Call and offer the Customer $15 off todays service for the inconvenience
Scuffed and fist size indented sheetrock damage reported by an Employee	Call the Customer immediately and let them know you will have it repaired. Let them know your handyman will reach out to get this fixed	Call and offer the Customer $30 off from their service to cover the costs of the damages	Tell the Employee not to worry about it
Customer completes a survey and says they did not feel like they got value from the service	Look over the job details and all the customers. Decide before the call if there was value, if the Customers reasons make sense offer them $165 refund to get them back closer to their original estimate	Look over the job details and all the customers. Decide before the call if there was value, if the Customers reasons make sense offer them $50 refund and a future credit of $50.	Call the Customer and let them vent Apologize profusely, let the Customer know you will use this as a training exercise.

I would say from this chart I am the throw money at everything fixer guy. There is nothing wrong with that and I can guarantee you it works, but if do not have the money to throw or give back, you will need to come up with other ways to make things right.

Sometimes a phone call from the owner of the business is enough to solve most problems. Customers feel especially important (as they should) when the owner of the business calls the Customer directly.

Showing empathy and taking ownership during complaint calls can help you completely avoid losing any money, (with most customers) and this may be your solution to the problems (especially if you cringe when money is returned to a customer)

You can also use the future service credits or better yet gift cards or certificates to your business. Offering a future service credit demonstrates to the customer that you accept responsibility for any errors made by you or your employees. This is a great tactic to retain a customer, save money on new customer acquisition, and avoid spending money you have already earned.

When you decide what part of the spectrum your solutions favor, you will be more prepared to use these solutions when issues arise. This will help you sleep better at night and not carry around the stress that comes with customer service issues.

Coming up with a Customer Service Vision

A **Customer Service Vision** is a statement that clearly defines the type of customer service employees are expected to provide. In some companies, this is a standalone statement that is separate from other items like mission, vision, and values. ... customer service standards.

A Customer Service Vision Statement should be everywhere, screensavers on computers, print-offs taped up in the work van and posted on the wall close to any phone you might use to speak with a Customer.

You should also promote your customer service mission on your website, social media, and even in your email signature. Customers will appreciate the attention paid to them and will be more confident in their hiring decision.

A few questions to ask when creating your Customer Service Vision Statement:

Who will we serve?
We serve our Customers or our Clients

What service will we provide them with?
What service does your small business provide to the Customer?

What can they expect from our service?
This is a great place to use verbs and adjectives that are dear to you. The best chimney cleaning, the best-looking lawn, or the top pest control

What are the focuses of your customers that should be incorporated into that vision? Are you ideal Customer budget-focused or quality focus? This could vary quite a bit depending on the business. For example, my carpet cleaning companies tend to be more about staying within the budget since it is a smaller and less invasive service. If they are hiring me through one of my moving companies, they are usually more focused on the quality of work, inquiring about things like insurance, and our employees' background checked.
Some of the past customer Service Visions I have used:

Moving Company: "We strive to provide our customers the safest and most organized moving service while maintaining your budget and expectations. "

Cleaning Company: "We aim to build a strong and profitable carpet cleaning service by always being fair, professional, and polite with our clients all the while providing them with the cleanest of cleans."

Remodeling Company: "Our focus is providing up to date well-crafted remodeling services while focusing on keeping to our customers budget giving our customers the most value for their dollar".

Creating a complaint process

A lot of complaints get blown out of proportion very quickly which is usually the result of bad processes or having processes that are not followed.

A customer is only going to call so many times and get sent to voicemail so many times before they start leaving one-star reviews online, bad-mouthing you on social media, and occasionally filing complaints with the state against your license.

A customer service issue must get treated with the same care as a new sales lead. They should be given priority over everything else on your to-do list for that day. Your reputation is online, and you cannot afford to lose time or money by having the reputation of your service business suffer.

I remember a little story that pretty much sums up customer Service and processes for most businesses. The story went something like this:

The man and his wife arrived at their favorite steak house in celebration of his wife's birthday. The steakhouse was known for having the best dry-aged cuts in town, as well as delectable side dishes. They sat for nearly 15 minutes before attracting a passing waiter's attention.

When they inquired about their waiter, the waiter apologized and stated that he would locate their correct waiter. After another 10 minutes, a waiter arrives at their table, his cigarette odor overpowering the pleasant aromas of dry-aged rib-eye cuts.

They place their order, and the food comes, one of the sides is wrong, the steak is well done and not medium rear like requested, and the other side was cold. It was their first bad experience at the restaurant, so they treated along trying not to let it ruin the evening. Dessert arrived, and the cake tasted weird that evening.

They got their check, paid their bill to the waiter, and started to leave the restaurant. As they walked by the hostess she stopped and thanked them: "Thank you again for dining with us. How was everything this evening".

The man looked at the hostess and replied: "Actually the service was way off tonight, and we had lots of wait time. My steak was cold, and I had one wrong side and the other side was cold. I also think they forgot to put the sugar in the cake frosting.

The man stared at the hostess expecting some story of empathy or resolve to his bad $186.54 steak dinner.

The waitress paused for another 20 seconds and then she said: "I am sorry Sir. They never taught me what to say after I asked that"

And this is the disconnect that I see in a lot of service businesses. No follow-up, bad if any customer service training and all, and a failure to remain enthusiastic about delivering the best service in your field.

There must be a strategy in place to carry out the operation. You and your entire team must be well-trained and familiar with the procedure, and you must adhere to it as closely as possible. It does not matter if you have twenty employees or if it is just you are working in the field and your wife answering the phone.

What if the young lady had responded with this instead? "Oh, I am so sorry that we seemed to have dropped the ball this evening. I believe I have seen you two in here before so that is completely unacceptable for our important customers. I know that was a lot of money to spend and not be happy, so may I get your name and phone number so I can relay this to my manager when she gets back in and we can get this addressed for you"

How much better would the customer feel. Would not just this little change in response keep these customers coming back? A sincere apology, taking ownership of the problem, and offering to make things right will please 95% of the customers out there (we will discuss the other 5% later in this book) and over half of that 95% will not even leave their name and number. Their desire to have the problem fixed was resolved with a simple statement with no mention of the words refund or future credit.

Let us look at this from a customer service process standpoint. What is the chain of events that should happen with this customer complaint? How do we ensure that customers who left their names and phone numbers are contacted, that their complaints are resolved, and that they are satisfied?

A good customer service process for this process might be:

If any persons have any interactions with any customers, they should greet them with a smile and make eye contact. If the opportunity arises after exchanging greetings, please inquire as to whether the Customer is enjoying their evening or whether there is something you can do to assist them. If things are not up to our standard by the response given, you can try and win the customer over by directly fixing the problem if it is within your capabilities and job duties. If not, please apologize for whatever issue caused the complaint and let the customer know you will retrieve a manager to come and get this addressed. There is no need to wait.

Some examples of some issues you may want to help address:

If someone needs a refill, please inquire as to what they were drinking and assure them know you will make sure that gets it as soon as possible. Let the waiter for that table or the floor manager know what drink the Customer needs, and politely identify them in the room without pointing.

If someone is upset about the service and seems ready to vent, feel free to let them vent and listen if your duties and capabilities allow. If you are not comfortable with solving this, please apologize to the customer and let them know you will get the manager right over to your table to get things resolved for them.

If a manager is absent or not on duty, please take their name and phone number and inform them that they will be contacted within 24 hours to make things right. Apologize that the manger is not currently on duty. Please text the information and specifics of the issue to the manager or your immediate floor supervisor.

When a manager receives a complaint, it should be followed up on within an hour whether the manager is on duty, or within the first hour of being on a new shift if the complaint was received off duty.

Any complaints that result in a refund for the meal should be documented in our CRM and noted in the credit card dashboard notes section.

If you offer a future service credit to the customer, issue them that amount in a gift card and cancel the charges. In the notes, please explain the reason for the card being issued at no charge. If the refund will be on their credit card, please let them know it will take 5-7 business days to appear. If they paid cash or through a delivery vendor, please let them know we will issue a check that will take 7-10 days to arrive.

If a customer threatens legal action or becomes enraged beyond control, please get them away from other customers as calmly as possible and let them know the owner will get this field and wants to speak with him or her personally. Let them know you will relay the message and I will call and feel comfortable to give them my name and cell phone number.

If we issue a mail refund, please email or text message the customer 7 days later to make sure the check arrived, or a credit card refund is posted. If everything is good there, ask them if they would like to lock in a reservation. If they decline, thank them and offer to handle their next reservation personally (this is a good way to plan to exceed)

Here are some examples of processes from my Moving Company and my Carpet Cleaning Companies:

Moving Company Complaint Process

Since we schedule our clients over the phone almost all our complaints and claims will be received over the telephone.
For Call Center Employees taking calls that are complaint or claim please follow these guidelines:

Apologize to the Customer for any inconvenience our service might have caused him or her.

- Let the Customer know you are going to transfer them to (use the Employees name) who will handle their issue. Let them know you will also email that person with the details and let them know that they will follow up within the day if that person schedule reflects otherwise (refer to general schedule)

- If this is a customer service complaint, please transfer them directly to the Operations Manager. Then send an email to the Operations Manager recapping what you know and include the Customers name and phone number. If the Operations Manager will be unavailable for a few days due to a holiday or long weekend, please email the Customer letting them know they will be contacted on that day. If more than a weekend and a business day, the complaint can be directed to a dispatch manager.

- If this is to file a new Claim please apologize and transfer them to the Compliance Department to get their claim processed. Please let them know you will also email the claims department and them if they do not answer or cannot answer

  If a Customer is extremely agitated or has called more than once with no contact returned, please ask them to hold and call the Operations Manager or the Dispatch Manager covering the Operations Manager schedule. Let them know you are going to transfer over to a Customer that has tried calling once already. Then let the Customer know you have updated the Operations Manager that we have dropped the ball twice and you are going to transfer them directly to him or her.

- After that contact, please send an email to Operations, Dispatch, and the owner on what you know about the call. In the subject line please put URGENT CUSTOMER SERVICE ISSUE. At all costs try to get a manager or owner on the line with the Customer. This is the last chance to pick up a dropped ball.

For my Carpet Cleaning Company which was a smaller operation we followed this process:

Carpet Cleaning Complaint Process

- When a new complaint comes in please apologize and take responsibility for the issue the Customer is reporting.

- Let the Customer know (use Agent's name) will get this resolved. Let them know he is in the field working and you will relay the message to call them back within the day.

- If the call sounds serious where the Agent may be the root of the issue, please notify Operations to get involved.

- If the Customer calls back because the agent has not made contact, please put the Customer on hold and connect them directly with Operations.

As you can see here having written processes that your employees can reference takes the stress off their shoulders and at the same time assures the customer that the complaint has been handled professionally and that it will get resolved. We must remember that your Window Installers may be able to do a takeoff for a 60-window home, they are unlikely to know how to deal with an irate customer if the windows arrive late.

As small business owners, it is our responsibility to train or allow other employees to train and continually train at making service a priority.

Your reputation around town will be one of the best in your industry and the referrals and word of mouth business will start pouring in on top of the higher conversions from jobs online because of wonderful reviews.

Preparing for a Customer Complaint call

The time has come. You have received the dreaded email, survey, or phone call from a customer that was not happy with a service you or your employees completed. Just like there is a process for reporting complaints, just as there must be a process for handling the complaint call.

If you receive a complaint call directly from the customer, remember to listen as they vent. When they are finished apologizing and let them know it is your job to fix it and you look forward to getting this addressed for them and be able to keep them as a customer long term. Let them know you need a little time to look over their account, job notes from Employees as well as touch base with the Employees. Ask them to give you a set time in the day.

For example:

"Mr. Neal, I apologize profusely for dropping the ball here. Can you please give me a little time this morning to look over your job details and notes and call you back at 3 pm promptly today to get this addressed for you"

Then as soon as you get off the call, set two reminders to call Mr. Neal back and get right on finding out what went wrong on Mr. Neal's job. Remember that customer service cannot take a back seat. As the Owner of a small service business or a manager of a small service business, those complaints always take priority.

You need to have a good work pad to figure out the best way to solve the customer service Issue you are addressing. You can use a notepad, but I would highly recommend making a sheet up that has all the details and can be catered to your business.

Using a form will help you draw out the problem, record the problem and hopefully resolve the problem. Having all the information available is a good way to work through the call.

You may want to have a couple of solutions ready to offer and for larger service businesses operations you may have a written scale with percentages or dollar value losses you aim for pre-set for employees.

Remind yourself before the call to watch out for any personal bad habits such as over-talking, getting angry or loud, or cutting the person speaking off before they finish. The call should not sound rehearsed, even though it is. The more natural you are with the call the better it will go.

Make sure you are in a quiet area and not rushed before you make the call. Breathe before you dial. Take deep 4 second breathes and exhale for 4 seconds and do this 4 times. Find your inner peace and pick-up the phone and dial.

This call might not go the way you are expecting. The solution that you find fair may not suit your Customer's idea of fairness. Do not go into the call carrying that thought on your shoulder. If that happens you will pivot and re-approach.

A good way to start the conversation may be:

"Good afternoon Mr. Neal. This is Jeremy just following up on the conversation we had this morning. I think I have some solutions to help you regain your trust in us. I apologize for the damage to your front door. I did speak with Randi and he told me he did accidentally bump the door with the large stand they were carrying, and it put the ding in your front door.

I reached out to the poor people and made them aware that you would be scheduling a time with them to get the door fixed and we will of course take care of the bill. Of course, if you have a couple of good days and times I can coordinate with the installer and confirm that with you. I know your time is valuable and I apologize you need to spend some of it with the door fix.

I would like to offer you a gift card with us for $75 off any future service. I want you to know I appreciate you allowing me to fix this mistake we made for you."

Doing this is not only the right thing to do morally it is also the right thing to do in business. Being fast to act to customer problems again is one of the most important parts of solving customer service issues.

Cleaning up any current reputation, reviews, and Customer Service Issues

You probably picked up this book intending to change who your business is. You are sick of the years of stressing over customer complaints and the fighting and arguing with your customers. It feels like you are in a bad marriage in dire need of some therapy.

Maybe by now, the damage has been done. As you google your business name and scroll around the internet you see the damage firsthand. Yelp 2-stars google 3.2 Stars, HomeAdvisor 3 Stars the list goes on and on with a hopeless about of feedback from customers over the years. Seeing the names, you even cringe as it brings back the memories of how the customer's issue was handled.

There is good news though. We can fix those reviews and the one we cannot fix we will soon drown out with all your new reviews.

First part first. This is not going to happen overnight, but it can be fixed in 3-6 months even if your online reportion is severely damaged. The good news is there is some things we can do immediately to start repairing your image online. The first thing you should do is respond to any reviews good or bad that are out there. If you have already responded, make sure the response fits these criteria if not click on edit and change it

- Make sure when responding to keep it short and sweet
- Just like in person, take ownership of mistakes and apologize
- Try to tuck some keywords in your review this is much easier with the good reviews for example:

  "Jamal, Thank-you for using us for your recent carpet cleaning. I appreciate your business and taking the time to leave us this review."

Responding to a bad review might look like this:

> "Cassie, I sincerely apologize that we dropped the ball on your move. I will be reaching out to you today to get this resolved or you can call me back at 843-000-0123. Thank-you for the opportunity to fix this"

Or,

> "Cassie, this should not have happened and is not the level of service I aim to provide. We should have made you aware that the job was going to cost more than expected and I look forward to getting the overcharge resolved. I tried reaching out with no response could you please call me back at 843-123-0000".

> And never, ever attack the customer personally online. You might think in your head that the response you gave them was good, but personally attacking a customer or airing out their dirty laundry will turn off more customers than it will bring in. It looks bad and immature and is at the bottom level of where your customer service skills currently are at.

Bad response from an owner would be:

> "Cassie, the bill was higher because you did not have anything packed so of course, it will take us longer if we need to do more work. You arrived late at your new house and my guys had to wait around almost an hour. The bookshelf was broken because it was old and made of a pressboard and was broken like that before we moved it. You should tell the whole story if you are going to spread lies online"

> Cringeworthy right? We have already other businesses and restraint reviews, and we have all seen the business owner who personally attacked the Customer online. Please be advised responding like the last response will kill your business, it makes

you look bad, and it is a bad habit that you can grow out of fast. It makes you look mad, and Customers perceive and business owners as bad business owners.

Having some 1 stars you would like to get rid of, it is possible to clean up those bad reviews so let us go through some ways we can get them removed and start rebuilding who you are as a company

How to get rid of bad reviews

How to start collecting new reviews is just as important as getting rid of bad reviews. The most powerful and fastest way you can improve your reputation fast is with more 4- and 5-star reviews.

1. Provide service that is worth 4-5 stars. It is possible and for owner-operators, there is no reason you can hold a perfect 5-star rating. Many of my service businesses have all perfect reviews across all platforms.

2. Have a CRM or website URL that screens reviews and catches bad ones before they post.
   Many CRMs now have an ask for a review feature as an add-on service. These services are indispensable and worth their weight in gold. What they do is automatically send Customers a request for a review via text message, email, or both. This is usually an automated task that we have to send 1 hour after the invoice is paid.
   The way the system works is at asks you to rate your service, if you pick 4 or 5 stars it re-directs you to the actual link you are promoting for a review. The best part though is if they leave a 4 star or let it brings them to a page where it asks, "Please tell us what went wrong" after the customer has rated below 4, they will then write what went wrong, now when they click the Next button, they will get this message: "I am sorry you were not

satisfied with our Service. I will be reaching out shortly to get this resolved. I appreciate the opportunity in making this right and look forward to getting any issue you may resolve"

This one feature with this one statement will stop the bad reviews. It gives the Customer a chance to vent and share that with you without beating you up online. I have yet to have a customer that got redirected to this review screener that went on to leave me real reviews where they count.

The only way you can mess this up is by not responding timely (I mean calling the customer within an hour of negative feedback (not review) received,) if you wait too long, the Customers anger will fester, and you will feel the wrath of that wait with the 1-star review notifications you will start to receive. The key is to respond fast and solve their issue quick

3. Change where reviews are harvested every 2-4 weeks. I like to rotate every 2 weeks and I shoot for 3-4 new reviews per week per location. For two weeks it will be Angie's List then it will be Home Advisor, then Google, then Yelp, then Facebook, and I will keep rotating around so that I am evenly distributing my reviews across platforms.

4. This helps give a much fuller picture to my Customers and from an online algorithm standpoint I am sure will help you rank better

5. Identify and start getting rid of current negative reviews.

The good news on top of your small service business's reputation improving quickly from your new flow of reviews from your new review plan, you also might want to take down some bad reviews based on technicalities or maybe they are from a former employee or even worse getting 1-starred by your competitors.

Some reason you can dispute or flag reviews for review:

- Most platforms will take it down if it uses derogatory language, conflict of interest, impersonating a person or if it has brand names in the review

- Left by a competitor is harder to prove but it does happen. When I fight these, I will submit screenshots of my customer list to show them that the Customer does not exist in my system and I suspect that it is one of my competitors. I have had several reviews from Google© over the years

Out of all the reviews, you can fight online you will find that Yelp will be the hardest (if even possible) and that Google will be the easiest, which is great because that is where 90% of service business online work comes from. With Facebook, you can remove the option to leave a review, which if you are trying to fix your reputation might be a good idea if it is lower than a 4.

This part may be the hardest pill to swallow, but when I tried this for one local service business, they went from a 2 star to a 4 star in a week. This is the other way to remove a review if you cannot get it removed on a technicality then it is time to dive into fixing it head-on.

The best way to fix things is to fix them right. This might cost a little money, but the return on investment will be more than you can imagine. You will feel a great weight lifted from your shoulders when you get them fixed.

Start reaching out to past customers through email or on the phone. I would highly suggest email as I have found that during these repairs it seems less aggressive because the customer is not put right on the spot lie, they would be if there is a phone call. If they do not respond to email then a phone call will suffice, use your best Customer handling skills when dealing with these hot potatoes though.

Explain to them that you are turning over a new leaf (do not mention you are trying to fix bad reviews) and that you know it has been a while, but you were hoping to make things right with the customer. If the issues were not handled the right way, you may want to appoint a manager to handle the peace offerings.

There are also third-party people you can find on Upwork © and Fiverr© that will handle the communications and fixes with these customers for a low rate. An email might look like this and all might go like this:

Dear Mrs. Jackson,

I know you used my services last year and that I dropped the ball on your service. Looking back at the issue and a year more mature in business I realize that how your issue was handled was incorrect.

I am trying hard to earn the trust back from Customers that I may have left behind. I would appreciate the chance to talk with you over the phone and get this addressed. If you are too busy to give me time now and would like to get this resolved via email, please let me know.

Looking back at the issue, it looks like we denied your claim for scratches on your dresser. I would like to either reimburse you for the damages or send my furniture repair guy out to get this fixed with you. I would also like to give you a $100 gift card to use with me in the future.

Let me know the best way to get this addressed for you. I appreciate your time and the opportunity to make this right.

Sincerely,
J Smith
Owner & Operator ILC Move

I know looking at it, that it is allotted to say. It takes a lot of personality and humility to fix these bad reviews. Remember do not offer to pay customers for fixing or changing their reviews. It does not excite people as much as you may think and it is against most platforms TOS and in some states, it's even illegal to leave false reviews, even if they are good.

Even enticing a Customer to leave you a 5-star review by offering something in exchange can get you banned online. A good way to get the review fixed is to email or call the Customer after the fix and ask them if everything is satisfactory (did the dresser get fixed? Did the refund check arrive?). If everything is ok and you can feel that the customer is truly satisfied, I would send an email that said:

Mr. Rand,

Thank you again for letting me get my mistakes with your service fixed. I have attached the $100 Gift Card as promised below. I hope in the future you trust to use us again for your floor cleaning.
I know there is a review online that I earned. If you get a chance could you maybe update the review to reflect my fix? This will help me earn the trust of other companies back.
When you need our service again, please email me directly so that I can make sure I send my best cleaners.
Thank you and I appreciate your business.

And that is it. It either works or it does not. 85% of the time customers will move the review to a 4. 15% of the time they leave it where it is. If they leave it where it is the only thing left, you can do is to respond professionally.

I apologize that we dropped the ball on your recent cleaning. I know since then we have recleaned those areas for you to make things right. I have used this feedback as a training tool for my Team. Thank you again for your business.

Be careful with rewarding employees for reviews. They should feel empowered enough to earn those reviews for themselves and the company. I even have a story about rewarding your employees for good reviews from their customers. Not even a week into offering a $5 per review earned reward did I find out some devasting news.
My top review earner, a middle-aged moving helper had been shoving his phone into the customer's hand with the site all pulled up to leave a review. He would put them on the spot to "earn" the review.

One customer a younger woman customer called after they left and told me how uncomfortable, she felt. I apologized and offered her a future move credit. I also sent her an email the next day explaining how I did this to improve my presence and I backfired.

Just another lesson from life while owning a service business.
Some good habits that align with exceptional customer service

- ✓ Answer the phone clearly with no background noise
- ✓ Properly introduce yourself and ask them for the customer's name
- ✓ Confirm all appointments via email and text message at the time of scheduling and 24 hours before any appointment
- ✓ Make sure any pricing on work orders or invoices is easy to understand. Not sure? Ask a friend or relative to review it
- ✓ Call or text 30 minutes before arrival
- ✓ Uniformed with the shirt tucked into form-fitting pants
- ✓ Walkthrough with the customer and explain your service
- ✓ Guarantee customers satisfaction
- ✓ Have the proper tools and wall/floor protection
- ✓ Do not charge a credit card fee – build it into your pricing
- ✓ Make sure the customer is happy with the work completed
- ✓ Accept Credit Cards, Cash App, Zelle, Venmo, and Crypto

BONUS – Top places Service Providers can get new work:

1. **Google Local** This is by far my favorite platform for all my service businesses. The leads that come through the Google Local Ads are the best of the best leads I have ever gotten online. You complete a background check; submit a copy of your insurance and you will see the leads start coming in on day one. (Check out my book Google Local Ads on Amazon, Walmart, or Google Play).

2. **Google Smart Ads** Another great Google product comes in second on my list. The Google Ads Smart platform is an automated platform that does not require you to spend the money on someone to manage your AdWords campaign. I found these ads go above national ads with Google using the most relevant algorithm to promote your business. With this platform, you can have top ad space for a 1/3 of what your competitors are paying.

3. **Facebook Ads** Facebook does work great. You must understand how it works though. People do not usually search for a service on Facebook so your ads should be promoting the idea that Customers need this service, I.E. (Do not let people talk about your Dirty Carpets, Facebook Special). Also, make sure you set up your Business Page on Facebook and make it shine.

4. **Google Maps** Google Maps is free, easy to use and once you rise from bottom to top will reward you nicely. Set up your service business on maps by visiting the Google my Business Dashboard. Uploads lots of pictures to this profile, and make sure you keep fresh reviews going through. Do not leave any information blank.

5. **Bing** It is not Google, but it costs a lot less as well. Bing will reward you with leads and calls for less. Bing has a smart option as well just like Google. One thing I have noticed is lots of my Angie's List and HomeAdvisor leads come from Bing, so if you do not use either of those service providers, you can still capture the work.

6. **Craigslist** If your new in business or are trying to get busier, Craigslist still works. Colorful ads, with emotions in the title, grab Customer attention, they do charge between $15-$15 per post in the service section. Some people complained about this, but I thought it was a good way to cut the cheaper guys off the platform.

7. **Instagram** I never thought Instagram would work for getting a new customer. But low and behold, with many of our videos getting over 10k views by using the words #satsifying when cleaning carpets or #satisfying when roller painting a wall or #satifying of a wall of boxes being loaded into a truck at high speed. Try and post regularly on here.

8. **Home Advisor** Ok, HomeAdvisor © can be a challenge. Their program is pay-per-lead. It does work, but there are a few things you need to consider. The first is how quickly can you respond and the second is to make sure your average revenue per ticket is at least $250. You will find you may get double leads through Angie's List and your Bing Ads, but if revenue is your goal ad it on.

9. **Angie's List** Angie's List charges a monthly fee for being on the "list". This is another one where your ticket price average needs to be in the two-hundred-and-fifty-dollar range.

10. **Email Marketing** No matter what your business, email marketing does work. Email lists for Realtors, Builders, and more can be

purchased online or mined yourself. Do not mass email. Email and introduction email 2-3 times per day just saying hello and telling them about your service. This is free and it works.

11. **Referrals** Referrals used to be in Networking groups through that has changed a little with COVID-19. You can get referrals from friends and family members and you can even offer gift cards or cash for people who refer work your way, in 2021 another great place to get referrals is by joining groups that need your service. You would be surprised how many Real Estate Groups post in the group asking for a referral.

12. **3 Up 3 Down** 3 Up /3 Down is a great cheap method for drumming up work. Get some door hangers or business cards made that say your just performed service at the neighbor's home and are offering all neighbors 10% off. After 6-8 months of doing this you will have 6-12 jobs a month flowing in from this (depending on the service you offer).

13. **SEO** Search Engine Optimization is the process of getting your website in the "natural" results on Google and Google Partner sites. It used to be expensive and had to be done by a pro. Many website builders and WordPress sites have added on where you can log in and blog daily, choose keywords and post pictures across multiple platforms. The one reason SEO is not as hot as it used to be is that the top fold of the website is filled with Ads and Map listings for almost all keywords.

14. **Blog Posts** Blog posts are a great way to get seen on the internet. Make sure your blog allows you to post on all your social media sites along with your WordPress Blog. Pick different topics. Not sure where to go with it? Search other blogs like your trade.

15. **Yelp** Yelp Customers are the hardest customers to please. I have found once you get past a 2-man operation it is hard to please Yelpers. A large portion of Customers from their platform want the best service for the cheapest price. I will say I own a one-man carpet cleaning company in Charleston SC, and he kills it on yelp. Yelp has a Pay Per Click option along with monthly charges for enhancing your profile.

Real Customer Service Stories

Again, this book is a guide on how to build a real Customer Service Culture at your business, the stories I have below are just a few of the hundreds of complaints I have dealt with over the years.

You may not like every way I deal with a problem, and that is OK, the common theme here is to put ideas and passion in your head about being a Customer Service Beast.

These stories may make you laugh they may make you cry, but I can assure you the problems and the solutions I used to fix them are all 100% real. Some names have been changed in these stories, but I can assure you they are 100% true. Use these stories and how I dealt with them to help you to deal with similar issues.

Customer missing large cash and coin collection

It seems like a lot of my stories come from Moving Companies. And you are right, there are plenty of stories I will be sharing with you that came from the moving business. It seems like out of all my businesses the moving company turned out the best stories.

This one story hit close to home and is a prime example of what can go wrong even when it is not your fault
This customer was a realtor who had been referring me work for years. She and her husband had decided to move from the south and go up north and hired us to pack up all their belongings and get them moved up North. This was a large ticket move for a VIP client and I sent a manager out to supervise the move from start to finish. This manager was related to me through marriage and had been working with me for years.

Again, the move was completed. The customer was happy, and I thought that would be the last time I would hear from them. A month later I get a call from the customer's husband. He was very polite and apologetic and told me a metal file box with over $20,000 in collector coins and bills with a value of over $100k was missing from the move. He was very humble and said he felt even bad making the call, but he remembers on the move day he went to tip the movers and my manager, and he says he remembers him being in a rush to leave. He said no one else had been in the home and he has checked every box and every room several times.
I let him know I would be getting this addressed immediately and let him know the Manger had been working for me for years and I could not imagine him doing anything like this.

The customer let me know the metal box was larger than a shoebox so I knew if this devasting news was true there is no way out of the three of them could they be in that small truck cab together and not see the metal box.

The next day after a sleepless night from my newest small business owner's stress I made my way to the office and had a long talk with the Manager and the two other movers. They all adamantly denied this and even said the Customer had tipped them over $100 each. They all swore that they not only did not take this metal box, but they also never saw the box.

I was beaten as I called the Customer back with the devastating news of my interview with my Employees. I asked him to please all and file a police report and that I would start the paperwork with my General Liability Insurance company to hopefully get him reimbursed for the collection. I knew it would not be that easy and the process would take a while.

I apologized again and let him know I would be working closely with the local police department to figure this out.

Three weeks later after many calls with my insurance company, my Customer, the police, and visits from the police at our workplace I received a call late at night from the Customer. I answered the phone thinking the worse.

"Jeremy, I am so, so, so sorry. I can't believe I put you through this," he started to explain himself, "I was just sitting in my office at the new house, and it hit me. I had put the metal box in the trunk of that old collector car I drove up here to this new home. I put it in there so the movers wouldn't lose it and I cannot believe I had this the whole time"

My jaw hit the floor. It was three weeks of stress that a family member might be stealing and working for you. While I was super relieved to have the guilt and responsibility off from my chest, it was a big lesson on how a serious customer issue I thought I and my Employees were responsible for in all actuality had nothing at all to do with me or my Team.

I followed the process that I had in place, but you can bet after this story I had disclaimers in all my Customers confirmation email and Bill of lading paperwork that they must declare anything of high value and that we were not responsible for any cash, jewelry or coins. Not because I do not trust my Employees, but because I know that part of growing and developing a business is trying to solve problems and create stops for those problems to arise again in the future.

On a side note, I appreciate the honesty with the Customer, I cannot imagine how hard it must have been to make that call to me that night.

Customer not happy with how clean carpets are after service

I own a few separate carpet cleaning companies and quite like moving companies I get a fair share of challenging Customer Service Issues. One day we got a call from a Customer that we had just serviced earlier in the day. The Customer said she is not happy with how her carpets came out and she does not feel like they are any cleaner than when they arrive.

I let the Customer know that we guarantee our work, and I would like the chance to make it right. I ask her if we can come out the next day and give it another try at getting clean.

I reach out to the first technician and ask him if he remembers the Customer. He said he does and that the floors had heavy traffic wear and the carpets had to be at least 20 years old. I ask him if he explained that when he did the walkthrough with the Customer and he said he had not explained that to her.

The next day I sent out a younger less experienced technician but who is a real technical person who is great with Customers. When he arrived, he told me the carpets had no hope. The technician took the time to explain the wear pattern on the carpet and how even if the caret did not appear cleaner her were cleaner with the steam and chemicals we use.

The technician gives the Customer peace of mind that she can even walk barefoot on some of the dark spots. While he was there, he cleaned her sectional sofa and ottoman for 20% off. He told me she still tipped him $50 on top of the billing he earned the company for the sectional clean. And that ladies and gentlemen are how good business is done and how a guarantee can make you money by giving your customer peace of mind.

Backing a pickup truck into a garage door

There will come a point in reading these stories where you might try and call me bullshit. You are going to think these stories are too crazy and could never happen. My only hope is that you can believe them because they are too wild to not be true. I had a small handyman and home remodeling business for several years.

I had one main carpenter working for me and he was an exceptionally reliable worker and great with our contractors. A garage door we had installed for a customer we had done a big remodel for the week prior was tight when you went to unlock it to open the door up. My carpenter went over, release some tension on one side of the springs showed the customer the fix, The Customer was elated for the quick fix and thanked the carpenter for the fix.
5 Minutes later the rear end of his 2007 chevy 1 ton was sitting in her garage, most of the new garage door laying partially in the bed of his pick-up. The customer snapped.

I am not sure what was going on in her life but having that truck in her garage with her brand-new garage door caved in was that breaking point. The lady called me yelling and cussing about how "dumb" we were.
I bit my tongue as I took a tongue lashing not even getting a chance to answer the calls from my carpenter that did the damage. After she slowed down her yelling and anger because I was not giving her any of my power and letting it upset me.

I drove right over to her home and the lady who was going to "kill" me a half-hour earlier humbly answered the door.
I apologized for the damage, drove up to Lowes, and repurchased the same door set and within 4 hours I and the carpenter had the door back together and fixed. The customer came out with two sweet teas trying to make peace.
This story is important for me, because

1. By me holding my composure and not playing back into the yelling and swearing I was able to bring my customer's temperature down as her bad behaviors could not outshine me keeping my composure.

2. I came to the customer's home. I found over the years I have been called every name in the book have been threatened with physical harm and more from customers. One thing I learned is if you go right to that customer's home (Not aggressively more like "Mr. Radcliffe I apologize that my Team dropped the ball today, this business is how I provide for me and my family and I can assure you I want to get this fixed. Could I come out and meet with you one on one tomorrow so we can talk this out and I can see the damage the mover's cause". Even now I use this line, no matter how mad the Customer is they calm it down about 90% when they realize I will be coming to deal with this face to face.

Every issue that arises will be a challenge, you will also get a feel for customers and what tactics work best with different personality types.

Disputed Credit Card Charge

If you take Credit Cards chargebacks are going to happen (c'mon Bitcoin!). I have had many credit card disputes over the years, and I feel like I have made the best I can out of what tends to be a bad situation. When you get the email that a dispute for a credit charge you made on a customer's credit card has been disputed it is hard not to get red-faced fast. The natural inclination is to pick up the phone and get your money by any means necessary. There are, however, better and more professional ways to deal with a credit card chargeback.

The first thing you should do is reach out to the Customer over the phone. While not the correct way to handle things, and illegal in most states (theft of services) some Customers will say they disputed because they are not happy with the service.

Normally if that is the reason and you have the correct paperwork (signed credit card slip, work order, recorded calls, etc.) you will most likely win the dispute with the credit card company.

The bad news is that if they disputed a credit card charge to deal with a customer service issue, to me this is only acceptable if they called in with the complaint and we failed t call them back. If it is the latter, they will probably be hell to deal with.

Maybe one and ten or twenty will ever pick up the phone after taking this route. If the Customer does answer focus on fixing the Customer issue rather than the payment. Two wrongs will not make a right, so be the bigger person and try and fix whatever their reported issue is. Then go back to getting paid.

First, complete and submit documentation on your credit card processer disputing the dispute. While this can take up to 90 days to resolve, (and they would remove the disputed amount the next day) normally I have found if they used service issues as the dispute reason you will probably win.

If after 90 days you do not win the dispute and or have not heard back from the Customer, you have a few other options to collect.

- First, send a letter for demand (you can do this before the dispute is resolved). Send it certified and professionally typed on letterhead. The letter could look something like this:

Dear Mr. Knowles,

My name is Jeremy Goding and I am writing to you in a reference to a recent credit card dispute you filed after receiving our services.

I have called, text message and emailed with no response and I really would like to get this resolved. The total due now is $235.35 for the fan we installed on March 8th.

I also live locally and was hoping we could get this resolved before I am forced to file a claim in small claims court and file a police report with the solicitor's office.

I hope we can reach some sort of agreement. I will even take payments if that makes it easier. You can call me directly on my cell at 843-000-9898 or email me at jeremy@kjkkl.com or send me a text message.

I look forward to getting this resolved and avoiding the headaches of the legal system. Thank you for your time and considerations.

- You can file a mechanical lien on the property even if the person who hired you does not own the home. In most states, this gives you and the homeowner time to work out payment before having to go to court to get lien added to the deed

- You can sue in small claims court for the dispute plus any court and filing costs. I have done this 3 times and all 3 times the Customer never showed up to court and a default judgment was ordered.

- Some counties will be able to contact the solicitor office who can pursue this criminal

Remember not to get your butt on your shoulders when dealing with these. As an owner, it is extremely hard to deal with customers trying to beat you out of money.

Bad driving reported in a company vehicle

The worst 1-star review is the one that you feel you did not earn. Having a company vehicle is a great form of advertising when your employees are heading to their jobs. It is also great if the owner wants to have his vehicle wrapped with advertising. I cannot count the times over the years that nice trucks with all the logos that cut me off in traffic, run a red light and almost hit me, or even give me the bird for driving too slowly, with the name of their business right there in front of you.

If you take a minute and look at some bad reviews online, you would be surprised how many small businesses (and large) have earned a 1-star review by driving recklessly or aggressively. It is important to know and remember that anytime you have a work shirt on or in a work vehicle you are representing the company to the public.

It is important for you and your employees to know and respect other potential customers and not just because it is good for business it is also the right thing to do. I would like to know if I had a driver driving recklessly, which is why we have Call Us Stickers on the back of all our trucks. A reckless driver can lead to a bad accident that can lead to huge increases in my commercial auto policy. Take the time and make sure safe courtesy driving is part of your training plan.

Employees smelling of drugs or alcohol

Of course, I will be going back to the moving company to share this story with you. A customer leaves you a review or completes feedback that says an employee or employee smells like marijuana or alcohol.

Let us be honest, the service industry probably has a larger share of drug and alcohol abusers than most "white collared" businesses. Some employees will have addiction issues others will just be caught up in that life.

Drugs and alcohol at work are a big no. I remember working for a landscape company in my younger years that had quite a few trucks and big contracts. The owners of the company would blaze up in the morning work truck with their employees.

I was amazed that it was even happening, and I am sure they feared some good help over the years that do not want to be around that environment. Nowadays we have states where it is even legal so that brings new challenges to the table

First, we will discuss how to handle with a customer and then we will talk about preventive issues in the service industry

This will be an awkward conversation with your Customer, but for me, the conversation went something like this:

"Hello Mrs. Tandem, this is Jeremy giving you a ring with Moving Company. I just saw your feedback that came in and I want to first apologize and tell you how embarrassed of this I am."

"I appreciate the feedback and wanted to let you know that we have no tolerance for that here. The two movers on your move are going to get a drug test and hopefully only one of them fails. Either way, I do not want you to think that is how we operate or that it will get swept under the rug. They were not working at full capacity, so I would like to refund you $250 and add a future $100 credit for helping us get to the root of the problem. I promise whatever action we take that neither mover will come back on your move and I will also not indicate at all it was from your move and I probably will tell a little fib to keep everything kosher and tell them someone at a gas station smelled it and called it in. I want you to be rest assured I am taking this profoundly serious."

Too many times in the service industry does this happen. Want to go out of business quick have a drunk employee run a pickup into the side of the school bus. You will be years digging out of that one and hopefully, everyone involved lives.

Some preventive measures I have used over the years that have had GREAT results in stopping use are:

- Owl Dash Cams © in the truck. Easy and cheap records inside and outside.

- Order professional Drug Free Stickers and Signs online and post them in the truck and shop

- Put up signs that say "Text 843-000-0000 to report any drug or alcohol use on the job. $100 Reward for reporting"

- In the back of our Moving Trucks, we put hunting cameras to capture activity in the back

- Do not allow ANY smoking in company vehicles

- Random Drug Tests for Drivers

- A Drug and Alcohol Plan – Just because an employee has a problem does not mean termination is the solution

- Train Managers and Supervisors to report and be aware of the smells and signs of drug and alcohol abuse.

This complaint can cost lives not only customer service issues. If you care about your business, your employees, and just your fellow citizens on the same roads, you will take this very seriously.

Minor present at the home

Want to avoid a bad situation that could make the news and even turn into a lawsuit? Enter a home where a minor is present and the trouble that could arise will scare you. Fortunately, in my younger days when I was into Cable Television Contracting, I learned the importance of following this rule.

It might be something you never even thought about. Your Employees in the field need to be made aware that if the person who greets you looks underage, confirm they are the customer, if they are not the Customer and say they are a child of the Customer, please confirm their age, if they are underage apologize and leave the residence and immediately call your supervisor or the owner and let them know what happened. Making this call will help falter and false claims that could arise.

We live in a world of lawsuits and I have heard horror stories about this one so makes sure you implement this into your training program.

The customer is extremely angry and threatening to sue or cause physical harm

We all have dealt with a hothead and if you are reading this book you might be one yourself. When you are dealing with a customer that is too angry to work with or threatens to sue you or cause physical harm, you are going to have to change the tactic a little bit. Remember 0 out of 100 customers that threaten to sue you will – LOL.

When it gets to this point and the conversation is not manageable, I would run with:
"Mr. Jimmy, I know you are upset, and I want to get this solved for you. If we cannot talk without the threats and the swears, we will need to disconnect the call so we can breathe a little and talk again later in the day. Can we get on the same page on respecting each other to get this solved?
And if Mr. Jimmy keeps yelling and swearing:
"Mr. Jimmy I am going to disconnect the call now. I will call you back tomorrow at 9 am when we both are composed. "

Property damage caused and not caused by your company

Crazy story from a small moving labor company that I owned way back in 2009. We provide services at an incredibly beautiful home and had a large crew of 6 movers on the job loading trucks all day at the home. The homeowner seemed extremely nice when I did a site visit and the crew told me later that he tipped them well.

A few weeks go by and I get a call from the customer telling me the crew scratched the floors all up when they were there.

Fast forward two months and the floor bill has risen to almost twenty thousand dollars, the guy was a renter, and the actual homeowner is a trial lawyer who sues the heck out of my insurance company. My insurance company hires a lawyer and I go to court as a witness on their side.

They selected a jury, and everything was serious. Halfway through the trial the renter is on the stand and admits that our team did not swap out the appliances that the renter (a professional chef) had swapped out when he moved there. He sold the appliances and the people who bought them came by with a couple of guys they found at a gas station and dragged the fridge and stove across these beautiful expensive floors. Then the renter's wife admitted on the stand they knew our movers did not cause the damage and her husband had already reached out to the people who bought the appliance about the damages.

The jury ruled in my insurance companies favor and this was after a full day in court. Every moving job after that we took pictures of the floors with our CRM time-stamped relieving us of paying for the damage we did not cause.

The customer was expecting more than previously agreed services

Last year I gave up on maintaining the shrubs around the big ditch in the corner of my yard. My wife saw a crew working at our neighbors and walked over and asked for a price.

The owner of the company walked over and told her $400. My wife thought that was more than fair and a few days later they came back and completed the work…. kind of.

The next day my wife went outside and saw only half of the bushes had been cut. The half that had been cut looked great, but the other half was still a mess. My wife called the landscaper and asked him why it was only half. The owner said he just did the half on her property. My wife explained we owned all the property around the ditch.

The next day the owner and his helper came out and finished cutting the rest of the shrubs on the other side of the ditch. My wife felt bad and gave the owner an extra $150, but it sounds like he should have charged at least 200 more.

Did you blame my wife when reading this? You should not. The homeowner explained the service she needs to be completed. The owner of the company should have given my wife an estimate in writing or emailed it over to her before starting the job with specific details.

Good documentation will save you thousands and maybe even tens of thousands of dollars a year. It may seem like a pain document so much, but here is just another simple example of a landscaper missing out on a new backpack blower.

The customer is going to file a complaint with the state reporting agency

I would rather a customer complaint end up in court rather than in front of a state agency. Whenever the licensing bureau or attorney general or consumer protection agency gets involved with a complaint it will most likely not end well. I take these threats seriously and it should hopefully not get to this point too often. Usually, the people who threaten are other small business owners who understand how reporting to agencies works and may use it as a leveraging tool to get what they from a complaint.

The customer wants to cancel and wants their deposit back

I get it. Customers canceling at the last minute can cost you money. You must know customers are serious about their appointment especially with larger services. I highly encourage taking a deposit on anything that makes more than one thousand dollars per job.

There will be times, maybe one in fisty when a customer demands their non-refundable deposit back. I know, I get it, its non-refundable, it is in the confirmation email and you told them on the phone. I will give you a head-up though.

If a customer is desperate enough to beat you up to get a non-refundable deposit back and do not get it, there will be hell to pay. Me personally, I just grit my teeth, tell them the refund will post in 5-7 days, and please call us if you need us or let your friends know about us.

Why cave in? Two reasons for me are I have been there, and it is also not worth a few 1-star reviews.

Customer calls looking for your employee(s) after the given arrival time

I spoke earlier about how we dwindled our late arrival calls earlier on in the book. You should not be surprised to hear that even with one-hour arrival windows once a month someone still misses getting there on time without contacting the office or the customer.

It is important to remember that we need to empower our employees to prevent issues from arising. This is more productive for you, management, and your customers. The rule of thumb at our companies is if we do not respect your time enough to call to say we were late; we should be monetarily penalized.

I would recommend that if you have a write-up policy in your employee manual that you give one verbal and then treat it as a serious write-up. Being late is a bad image.
As an owner, you need to manage time and being on time for yourself and your employees. In the event your mis a deadline or appointment time, it should have been communicated to the customers hours in advance versus when the customer calls the office looking for their technician.

As I mentioned earlier if you need to change some operational processes (1-hour arrival windows in the morning and 2-hour arrival windows in the afternoon) go ahead and do it. The mission here is to prevent issues before they arise. Try it out for a while and you will thank me for it.

Accusations of medication, cash, or jewelry being stolen

Stolen medication, watches, baseball collections, cash and unfortunately an AR-15 gun. Even with background checks (most of them military base approved), things came up missing and lots of time it was my employees who were guilty. Allot of my operations have 20+ Employees and I have had up to 160 employees on the ground at one time.

I just wanted to give you those numbers to put into perspective how many people we were dealing with and not that I just was hiring the worse of the worse. I learned in life to meet good people you will need to meet a lot of bad people. My first theft story goes back to 2009 for another moving company I owned. We performed a move for a gentleman, and he came by our office the day after the move in a frenzy.

Noticing he was upset I asked him if I could help him, and he started to tell me his issue. On the move yesterday he thought everything went well until this morning when he started looking for his work laptop.

The gentleman had worked for a large cellular company and had a huge presentation that he had been working on for months. The entire project was on an SD card and that is all he wanted back. They can keep the laptop he said.

I immediately got the crew into my office and one of the older guys called out the young clean-cut kid who would have been the last person I ever would have guessed to take it. The kid broke down crying like a baby and we followed him out to his car to retrieve the laptop with the SD card in place. I was humiliated and refunded the man's entire move cost in full. I then called the police, but the customer would not press charges…. wish I would have known that before an $800 refund.

The pill epidemic has overtaken the service industry. It is a whole new thing to look out for its easily hidden and there is no way to judge who does pills. One of my carpet cleaning customers came into the office ranting and raving that her carpet cleaner stole her medication.

The cleaner was already on another job, so we had a supervisor go out and site visit and help the accused employee finish the other clean. In the meantime, back at the office the customer who was quite wired for sound was accusing the cleaner of taking a bottle of pain pills.
By this time in life not how much liked an employee I would also not put anything past anyone. I called the local police department at the customer's request to file a report and they came by she was agitated and high on something.

A few days later the local investigator came by the office after speaking with the carpet cleaner who swore it was not her.
Well, to make a long story interesting the investigator told me the lady who accused the cleaner of stealing the pills had most likely abused the pills herself and filed the report in hopes of getting her physician to refill the prescription.

Unfortunately for her the doctor spoke with the investigator and let the investigator know that the woman was seriously addicted to pain pills. Just another crazy story that is so senseless it makes sense.

When reflecting on these two stories I just want you know that there is never a real clear path in theft situations. They are touchy and humiliating to deal with, but honesty and getting the proper authorities involved will help you prevail.

Mis-scheduled job

It happens to the best of us. I remember when I had a flip phone and a notebook that I would do my scheduling in. There was that breaking point as my business grew where I was transitioning between a notebook and my new CRM. During that transition in less than a year, I was pushing over a million a year in revenue.

It was a busy Saturday morning, and I had all 6 of my trucks lined up and ready to go. It was going to be a great day with 10k of moves on the books. All my team shows up on time, wide awake and ready to go, the last truck rolls out the gate at 8:15 am.

8:55 am the phone rings and I get ready for my first sale of the day...

"Jeremy, this is Mr. Carroll, I was just calling to see where the trucks are at. I know we had an 830 am appointment so I am wondering if they got lost in the neighborhood?"

Now my jaw hit the ground. Mr. Carroll was my 2 Truck six-thousand-dollar local move. It was at that moment I remember writing Mr. Carroll's appointment into my schedule book after completing his in-home estimate.

I also at that moment remembered I did not enter Mr. Carroll's job into the new CRM I started using. Mr. Carroll, a huge job, must be out today has closing Monday morning with a walkthrough Sunday afternoon. Suddenly my day of glory has turned into a pile of turd.

When situations like this arise, it is your job as an entrepreneur to react quickly, come up with a plan and minimize reputation and financial damage.

I made the call and pulled two trucks off their other smaller jobs for the day and redirected them to Mr. Carroll's move and prepared for the phone calls I had to make to the two moves I would not be able to cover that day. I picked up the phone and dialed the first customer. After no answer, I went on and called the second customer. This customer lived in a large apartment and his lease was not over until Tuesday.

I apologized and let him know I had dropped the ball and over-scheduled the route. I offered him 2 free hours ($300) on his move if we could push it until the next day. I tried calling the first customer again and no answer. The customer never called me back and the deeper into the ticket I looked I saw she was wishy-washy when setting the appointment. So, for $300 I was able to save face on a $5900 move (I gave Mr. Carroll a $100 credit for us being late), and the day's revenue ended up at almost 14k!

Thinking too long could have cost me with this one. The team was within 5 miles of the gentleman who we rescheduled. It would have been too late to redirect them if they had already arrived. Also, do not let the thought of losing a few hundred dollars cost you thousands.
I see too many business owners trying to be cheap and it bites them in the butt. Like one person who purchased one of my companies the first thing he did was stop accepting American Express because their processing fees were too high. At least that is what he saw. What I saw was someone who cut out some of the best customers he could have kept.

And I got lucky with the lady who never called me back.

The customer is overly emotional and maybe a little "off"

There is one thing that I realized. Some people are just bat shit crazy. I have dealt with some wonderful people over the years, but no joking around I have had some customers so mentally checked out that it makes me nervous knowing they operate a vehicle on the same road as my wife and my daughter. When you come across someone who is dealing with mental or emotional issues your strategy with any issues they may have must be handled with care. You may need to bend more than usual and try to find compassion with their current state of mind.

Employee injured (or worse) at customer's home

I hate telling this story as it was a devasting day for me. A gentleman came in for an interview for a driver at one of my moving companies. He was hired on the spot and that afternoon went to the urgent care to get his D.O.T. Physical. The man had been out of work for years and I remember how ecstatic he was when he got hired.

The next day he came for his first day. He would be training under another team for a couple of weeks. The crew headed out that morning and the new guy was eager to go and learn.

At 10 am that morning dispatch gets a call that the new guy died. Obviously, we were shocked and did not even think it was real, but even af6er seeing a doctor the day before for a medical evaluation, the young man who was on 32 years old had a heart attack and died not even an hour into starting the job.

This was a severe case that affected me for a long time. You always feel a sense of responsibility for those who work with you and I even had to break the news to the young man's father.

The customers who were moving out were quite devasted and concerned as well. There was no anger from the customer on this one more just concern and worry. Believe me, though the wrong customer would have turned this into a refund opportunity.

While you hopefully will never have to deal with that, you may still have employees in the service business passing out from the heat, cutting fingers with a chainsaw, putting a nail through your knuckle with a pneumatic nail gun, and hundreds of more crazy incidents.

I even once had an employee that goes so dehydrated, he hallucinated and got naked at the customer's home and jumped into a pond behind the customers' home.

Each case will be different, but I have found customers are understanding that accidents happen. What they are not understanding is who is going to pay the bill. If you have workman's comp email a copy of the accord with a short email letting them know the person is an employee and your insurance will handle it. If you don't have workman's compensation send a nice apology email with a hard copy of your General Liability accord and let them know you are responsible for your employee. Give them peace of mind that they will not be liable for any cost related to the injury.

Customer complains of bad behavior from an employee

From customers accusing employees of hitting on them to swearing in front of the customer, bad attitudes, and even an accusation of "blowing up" the bathroom.
While there is probably no written process on how to handle a customer complaining about an employee going #2 in their bathroom, it is important to understand that most of these problems are interchangeable issues that can easily have the same issue.

For example, A customer just called and said, "Mark your cleaner just <u>swore</u> in front of me". The underline can be interchanged with many similar bad behaviors meaning for most art they will have similar solutions. You could use: "Mark your cleaner <u>was rude</u> to me" or even "Mark you cleaner just <u>took a personal call</u>-in front of me"

One of my first moving companies employed a variety of unique characters. Some of my most challenging "bad" behaviors came from 2009-2014 while operating my first moving company.
I had a great employee who was a driver and had been with the company a little over a year. Like most o the crew, he was a little rough around the edges, but customers always loved him, and I do not recall a rating ever below four stars. This employee was tall, dark, and handsome and the worst part was he knew this.
One day we get a call in the office from a customer of this employee from a week or so back. The customers were a husband and wife moving from an apartment into a new home.

The husband had called in irate and demanding to speak with this employee now. He was so excited by the time the call got to me I had to take a moment and ask him to breathe and to try and bring his excitement down so I could understand him better.

The story went like this. On the move last week this driver and the customer's wife were getting might friendly. Sometime during the move, they got too friendly and exchanged a kiss in the master bedroom closet. After the move, they stayed in touch via text message.

Not only was the customer married, but so was the employee. As it came to light the employee's wife was going through his phone and found messages between this employee and the customer's wife. His wife then proceeded to show up at this new customer's home (not sure if she got the address from her husband or his schedule on this smartphone) calling out the lady into the front yard to fight.

The door never opened, and the police were called. As this employee's wife was getting arrested in the customer's yard the story came to light about how the customer's wife and the mover had been "sexting".

The situation got bad quickly and the customer was demanding a full refund. We ended up agreeing on refunding half the move (his half) and shortly after his wife called in for movers. We politely declined in trying to avoid a domestic violence issue and a few weeks later the stellar employee's drama caught up with him, he was arrested and since it was assault was not allowed back at work.

Reflecting on this story I realized that even with a situation that seemed as unpredictable as that one I still needed to claim responsibility.

I had been hearing movers talk about how this employee had been friendly with customers in the past. I had even heard of the phone number exchange with prior customers (yes, this fella had charm) and I just let that info go in one ear and out the other.

This is one of those stories that taught me to listen better to the gossip of the employees. Had I been more proactive in addressing this unprofessional exchange with this employee I may have saved this employee's job, the money it cost to train him, the money it cost to refund the customer's husband, and who knows maybe even save a marriage. Many "bad" habits can be picked off before they are happening or at least happen again.

It is easy as a small business owner to get frustrated with stories like this. I agree, but I also know it is not much you can do about the past. There is however something you can do about the future. In every employee training manual in every service business that there was always a section about avoiding personal contact with customers during work or even after work.

Dealing with Covid-19

2020 brought with it the biggest challenges I and many others have ever faced as a small business owner.
The safety issues with COVID-19 for myself, my employee, and my customers were directly put on the line.
That on top of the political spectrum and I had a few unique customer service issues arrive that I would never have expected in 2020.

As a rule, no matter if you understand science or not should be to keep your employee always masked. Hand sanitizer in work trucks, replacing masks with new or clean ones, and making sure any equipment that goes from home to home is cleaned well with a germicide to kill the Covid-19.

It is your responsibility to keep your employees and your customers safe and at the time of publishing this book, there was no lawsuit protection in place for small business owners.

Taking the time to train your employees for the new world of Covid-19 and new airborne germs on the spread is an important part of keeping your employee and customer safe as well as keep the peace with your customers. Some topics you might want to touch on that some of my businesses have encountered would be:

- If a customer gets upset that your employee is entering the home "masked"
- What information you are giving the customer before they arrive
- How to work safely in the world of COVID-19
- How to access PPP Gear
- Reimbursements for PPP gear

Hopefully by the time you have read this book that this has passed, and we can get vaccinated and move on.

Build a Customer Service Manual

Writing down your customer service procedures and the process is especially important as you grow your business. If you have everything organized and printed in a three-ring folder next to anyone that will handle customer calls you will see your stress level and the stress level of the employee handling complaints drop significantly.

This book will be the go-to guide for you and your employees and managers as you grow. It should be well organized; the type is written and be updated as the process change. A few key sections to have in your Customer Service Manual would be:

- Copy Customer Service Vision
- Copy of Customer Complaint Worksheets
- A list of vendors used for repair support
- A list of the top 25-50 common issues and the most common recommended solution

Document your issues well and how you solve them better. Using this guide will reduce costs and service issues for years to come.

I would highly recommend taking your top 25 complaints and break them down into a FAQ, so you have plans for dealing with common customer service issues. And as always you should be focused on creating processes that can cut that list in half.

Into the future...

As the owner of a small business, you will have lots of customer service challenges. As the owner of a small business that is a service business, you will have even more customer service challenges. Knowing that you are taken the time to study and learn how to improve your customer experience says a lot about the company you will become.

I hope you find the information in this book helped create a better feel for the customer experience and a better way to prevent issues from arising. The ability to let go and have a process in place that will protect you is a good feeling. Providing exceptional customer service and having great reviews across the internet outweighs a big bank balance any day. I can assure you if you provide one the other follows naturally.

About the Author

Jeremy Goding is a sales coach, published author, and owns and operates 4-6 service businesses across two different states at any given time. Jeremy has been featured in Inc and Entrepreneur Magazine and has had several successful service businesses started with just him and developed into multimillion-dollar operations. Jeremy is supported by his wife of almost 20 years Keisha Goding and his two beautiful children Riley and Brooke. The family loves their dogs, travel, and good food. You can contact the author with questions at jeremy@jeremygoding.com

Back Page

1Are you tired of searching for the right book on how to better your customer's experience with your business?
Do the books you come across only seem to cover customer service issues at banks, grocery stores, and other "white collared" workplace settings?

Being in the service business my entire life while owning and still owning several service businesses from moving companies, carpet cleaning companies, handyman businesses, and more I have come across the REAL customer service issues that Service Businesses deal with.

In this book, I share my experience with the "real" Customers we deal with in the service industry. I will share my methods and ideas to help you home in on being the 5-Star Service business you know

www.ingramcontent.com/pod-product-compliance
Lightning Source LLC
Chambersburg PA
CBHW071026220526
45467CB00004B/1518